The EXECUTIVE BRANCH

The
EXECUTIVE
BRANCH

by Diane Patrick

★ ★ ★

Franklin Watts
New York / Chicago / London / Toronto / Sydney
A First Book

Cover photograph courtesy of The White House, Counsel to the President
Photographs copyright ©: Archive Photos, NYC: pp. 6, 56 (both R. Thompson),
12 (Lambert), 13; National Archives: p. 10; North Wind Picture Archives, Alfred, Me.:
p. 10 insert, 11; The Bettmann Archive: p 14; The White House: p. 17; Wide World
Photos: pp. 18, 24, 33, 36, 38, 43; U.S. Army Photograph: p. 20; Gamma-Liaison:
pp. 21 (Brad Markel), 28 (Dirck Halstead), 47 (Renato Rotolo); UPI/Bettmann:
pp. 22, 23; Jay Mallin: pp. 27, 40, 41; LBJ Library/Cecil Stoushton: p. 31; Delmarva
Poultry Industry Inc.: p. 37; NOAA: p. 39; Tennessee Valley Authority: p. 44; U.S.
Department of Health and Human Services: p. 45; U.S. Department of the Interior:
pp. 48, 49; The Library of Congress: p. 51; New York Public Library, Rare Print
Collection: p. 53 top; U.S. Department of Labor, OSHA/E. Latour: p. 53 bottom;
United Nations: p. 54; U.S. Bureau of Engraving and Printing: p. 57.

Library of Congress Cataloging-in-Publication Data

Patrick, Diane.
    The executive branch / Diane Patrick.
    p. cm. — (A First book)
    Includes bibliographical references and index.
      ISBN 0-531-20179-1
      1. Presidents—United States—Juvenile literature. 2. Cabinet officers—
United States—Juvenile literature. 3. Executive departments—United States—
Juvenile literature. [1. Presidents. 2. Cabinet officers. 3. Executive department.]
I. Title. II. Series.
JK517.P38 1994
353—dc20   94-963
                      CIP
                      AC

Contents

The president both works and lives in the White House.

Introduction

The United States is a big and complex country that has millions of citizens. It also has millions of square miles of land: fifty states plus several outlying territories, including more than two thousand tiny islands scattered throughout the Caribbean Sea and the Pacific Ocean.

All of the citizens of the United States and its territories are governed in an organized way, and have been for more than two hundred years, by a system of government that the people of the United States created back in 1787.

Many of those early Americans had come from England to start new colonies, which were kind of like branches of Great Britain or England. But after a few years the colonists became unhappy with the way they were being treated by their ruler, the king of England. In fact, they grew so unhappy that they decided to change the way they were governed. So the leaders of the colonies met and decided to set up a better system of government.

Theirs was a simple system. It was based on the idea that the people should govern themselves instead of being ruled by a king. The colonial leaders carefully devised a plan of government where power could never be in the hands of any one person, like a king or a queen. Under this new system, the most important governing responsibilities were making laws, interpreting laws, and enforcing laws. Thus, the government of the United States was, and still is, separated into those three parts.

This book will tell you something about the executive branch, one branch of that three-part system of government.

Chapter 1

How the American System of Government Began

For hundreds of years now, brave citizens all over the world have stood up to governments they used to be afraid of. This has happened in countries where kings once ruled, and it has happened in countries where presidents ruled. It is still happening today in many countries all over the world. And that is how the United States of America was born.

In 1607, Great Britain began to set up colonies on the eastern coast of North America, by the Atlantic Ocean. Even though they were far away from England, these colonies were still considered a part of Great Britain, and therefore they were under the king's rule.

By the middle of the 1700s, there were thirteen of these British colonies. The people in the colonies were thinking and living differently than people back in Great Britain, the mother country. The colonists were also very unhappy with the way they were being ruled by the king. Finally, in 1775, the colonists went to war against Great Britain. This war was called the American Revolution, or the Revolutionary War. By 1781, Great Britain had lost this war, and the king no longer had control of the colonies.

The Declaration of Independence

In 1776, early in the Revolutionary War, the colonists decided to declare their independence.

Thomas Jefferson put the people's wishes into a document called the Declaration of Independence. That document is a very important part of American history.

The Declaration is written in words that are very easy to understand. It has three parts. The first part, the Preamble, expresses the people's belief in democracy, or rule by the

The Declaration of Independence, written by Thomas Jefferson, set forth in three parts America's democratic beliefs.

Representatives from the American colonies risked their lives and property to sign the Declaration of Independence shown here in an engraving made from a famous painting by John Trumbull.

people. The idea of rule by the people was an amazing one at that time. In those days, countries were ruled either by kings or by aristocrats—people who had been born into powerful noble families. But the colonists had decided that it was time to change.

So the first part of the Declaration of Independence stated that "all men are created equal" and have "certain unalienable rights." It also stated that when rulers refuse to grant the people those rights, the people have a right to get rid of the government.

Birth of Our Nations Flag.

The myth of Betsy Ross and the sewing of the first American flag is one of the most enduring tales from the American Revolution.

The second part of the Declaration is a long list of complaints against George III, the king of England.

The third and final part of the Declaration of Independence states that the colonies were now free and independent and no longer loyal to the British king. The document was signed by fifty-six representatives of the colonies.

This statement of the people's rights and of their intention to rule themselves had a tremendous effect throughout the world back then. It inspired the French people, who in 1789 overthrew their king, Louis XVI. It encouraged Latin American leaders, such as Simón Bolívar, José de San Martín, and José Martí, to fight for independence from Spain.

Simón Bolívar

Even now, more than two hundred years later, people all over the world are inspired by the Declaration. Recently, African, Chinese, and Russian people have fought for independence.

By winning the Revolutionary War, the colonies became independent states. They joined together and called themselves the United States of America. The next question was, how would the new nation be governed?

It took almost twelve years of thought, discussion, and debate for the states to decide on a system of government. Finally, a constitution was written in 1787. It states the rules and principles of the American system of government.

The Constitution is a document that tells how the United States is to be governed. It was written very carefully, because the people knew that any government with too much power could be dangerous. Too strong a government might become a tyranny, like the British rule the Americans had recently escaped.

The Constitution was written by representatives from the thirteen states. It allowed for government decisions to be made thoughtfully and discussed thoroughly.

The Bill of Rights is a document that added the first ten amendments to the U.S. Constitution in 1789.

It also allowed for change, and it was designed so that no government decisions could be made by one person. Most of the government power was given to the states and to the people in them.

To make sure that this would work, the writers of the Constitution created three branches of government. The first branch is headed by a president and is called the executive branch. The second is headed by Congress and is known as the legislative branch. And the third is headed by the Supreme Court and is called the judicial branch. No one branch of the government has more power than the others.

Chapter 2

The President

The president of the United States is the head of the executive branch of the government. That is why the president is also called the chief executive.

The executive branch is made up of the president and vice president, of course. Another part of this branch is the Executive Office of the President, which is a team of the president's closest advisers. The cabinet is also part of the executive branch. It is made up of the chiefs of all the government departments.

Many things about the president's job have changed since George Washington, the first President of the United States, was in office.

George Washington, who was the chief executive from 1789 to 1797, had to find his own place to live. Today the president lives and works in the White House.

George Washington's cabinet had only four members. The cabinet of President George Bush had more than thirteen members.

George Washington himself answered all of the official letters he received. Today the White House receives millions

The Oval Office in the White House as it looked during President Bill Clinton's first year in office.

While most presidents have had relatively small staffs, those in office since World War II have needed many more people to help run the Executive Branch.

of letters every year, and many staff members are needed to answer them.

George Washington often traveled alone and made most of the travel arrangements himself. Today the trips are planned by experts, and the president never goes anywhere alone.

The presidency is a very important position. But both Congress and the Supreme Court can limit the president's power. Some of the chief executive's powers are formal—that is, they are granted by the Constitution. Others can come from acts of Congress. Also, Congress can give the president emergency powers in times of national crisis.

Other powers of the president are *informal*—that is, they arise from custom or simply from the status of the president's position.

These are the formal powers granted to the president by the Constitution:

1. The president serves as commander in chief of the armed forces.

2. The president appoints the head of each executive department and requires all department heads to turn in reports.

3. The president can grant pardons for crimes.

4. The president can make treaties, with the agreement of the Senate.

5. The president can appoint ambassadors, Supreme Court justices, and other officials, with the advice and consent of the Senate.

6. The president can appoint high-ranking officials to fill vacancies when the Senate is not in session.

7. The president must inform Congress from time to time about the state of the Union, and recommend new laws.

8. The president can call either house or both houses of Congress into session.

9. The president can receive ambassadors and other representatives of foreign countries.

10. The president sees to it that the laws of the United States are enforced.

11. The president commissions all officers of the United States.

One of the president's most important powers is to act as commander in chief of the military. Here, President Franklin D. Roosevelt signs the resolution that formally put the United States at war with Japan in December 1941.

Under the Constitution the U.S. president must address the joint houses of Congress and inform them of the state of the union. Here, President Clinton exercises his constitutional right and duty.

Campaigning for the presidency is filled with posters, buttons, television ads, parades, and nearly any other effort that candidates feel will result in their election to the country's highest office. (Above) The 1968 Democratic convention nominated Hubert Humphrey as its candidate. The convention was marked by anti–Vietnam War riots in the streets of Chicago. (Right) Eight years earlier, John and Jacqueline Kennedy received a joyous reception in a ticker tape parade through the streets of New York City after his nomination as the Democratic candidate.

In the event that a president cannot fulfill his term of office, either because of illness or death, the vice president assumes the presidency. Here Harry S. Truman is sworn into office after the death of Franklin D. Roosevelt.

The Constitution requires that the president be at least thirty-five years old. He must have been born in the United States and a resident of the United States for at least fourteen years. The same requirements apply to the vice president, who could become president.

The president is elected by the people of the United States for a four-year term. The Constitution says that a president cannot serve for more than two terms. The president and the vice president are sworn into office in an inauguration ceremony held on January 20. Both have power to act as soon as they are sworn in. The Constitution says that the president should be paid, but the amount of that payment is decided by Congress.

The president is also provided with a home and a staff to take care of the building and grounds. When the president and his family want to go away to relax, they are allowed to use Camp David, a U.S. government facility in the mountains of Maryland. Protection for the president and the president's family is provided by the Secret Service.

The vice president is also paid a salary and receives an expense account. The vice president also is provided with a residence, the vice-presidential mansion.

Former presidents, too, receive a salary and a budget. With this money they hire a staff to help them with such things as correspondence and speeches.

Chapter 3

The Executive Office of the President

T he staff of the president has a very big job. Its members must keep in touch with the individual members of Congress, the heads of executive agencies, the media, and the general public. And they must also serve as advisers to the president.

The advisers who work directly for the president are those in the Executive Office of the President. Each president personally decides how the executive office is to be organized, so it may change with each new president.

The executive office may include:

1. The National Security Council advises the president on matters relating to the country's safety. It is most concerned with foreign policy—that is, the rules for dealing with other countries. The council is made up of the president, the vice president, the secretary of state, and the secretary of defense. Advisers who often help the council include the director of the Central Intelligence Agency (CIA), the chairman of the Joint Chiefs of Staff, and the special assistant to the president

Presidential adviser George Stephanopolous is an example of the relative youth of President Clinton's staff.

for national security affairs. The president may also invite other people to participate.

2. The White House Office has the most responsibilities. It usually includes several dozen personal aides to the president, plus their aides. Also on staff are many stenographers, messengers, and secretaries, who handle the huge amount of mail that the White House

Henry Kissinger (left) was perhaps the most famous national security adviser. He went on to become President Richard Nixon's (right) secretary of state.

receives. By doing all this work, these people keep the president free to work on more important problems.

3. The Office of Management and Budget prepares the federal budget each year, deciding how much money each agency will be allowed to spend. It reviews the budget requests for each agency and holds hearings so that officials from each agency get a chance to argue in favor of their budgets.

4. The Office of Policy Development advises the president on how to deal with the nation's problems at home.

5. The National Critical Materials Council makes sure that the United States has enough of the important materials it needs for industry and national security. This council also makes sure that the nation keeps up with the latest technology concerning these materials.

6. The Council of Economic Advisers helps to solve major economic problems. It is made up of three economists who advise the president on ways to keep the nation's economy healthy.

7. The Council on Environmental Quality advises the president on methods the government can use to control pollution. Sometimes the council suggests laws that Congress might enact and executive orders that the president might issue.

8. The Office of the United States Trade Representative is headed by the special representative, an official with the rank of ambassador. This official is in charge of working out trade agreements with other countries.

9. The Office of Science and Technology Policy gathers information on science, engineering, and other technology for the president.

10. The Office of Administration provides general office services for the executive office of the president.
11. The Office of National Drug Control Policy coordinates federal, state, and local efforts to control illegal drug use. It also develops antidrug activities.

The Vice President

The vice president is elected at the same time as the president and serves the same term of office. The writers of the Constitution created the office of vice president so that someone could automatically serve as the president if the chief executive died or resigned.

The Constitution gives the vice president only two duties: (1) to preside over the Senate, and (2) to help decide when a president is too disabled to perform the duties of office.

Some presidents, however, give the vice president additional responsibilities, such as presiding over the meetings of the cabinet and making goodwill trips abroad.

The nation came to a complete halt after President John Kennedy's assassination in Dallas in 1963. A Texas judge swears in Vice President Lyndon B. Johnson as his wife, Lady Bird (left), and the president's widow, Jacqueline Kennedy, look on aboard the presidential jet, Air Force One.

Chapter 4

The Cabinet

The cabinet is made up of the department heads of the government departments of the executive branch. Within these departments, there are hundreds of agencies and bureaus. Many departments run programs that help the American people.

The number of departments depends on the things that are happening in the country during a president's term of office. Some departments have existed since George Washington's time. Others were established much more recently. Over the years, some departments have changed their names to reflect social changes or new ways of thinking.

Sometimes when people talk about these departments or the agencies in these departments, they simply call them "the government."

The head of each department is usually called a secretary. The secretary is appointed by the president and confirmed, or approved, by the Senate. Together these department heads, as we said above, make up the president's cabinet. The cabinet serves as a team of advisers to the president on important national and international issues.

Each department of the Executive Branch is headed by a secretary. Together these department heads make up the president's cabinet. Here, President Clinton meets with his cabinet members.

The cabinet is not actually mentioned in the Constitution. But President George Washington started the tradition of meeting with the heads of executive departments and listening to their advice.

The cabinet members do not usually work directly with the president every day. They are busy running their departments, which employ thousands of people.

The vice president also participates in cabinet meetings. Other individuals are often invited to participate in discussions of particular subjects.

Fourteen departments are now represented in the cabinet. They are:

1. Agriculture
2. Commerce
3. Defense
4. Education
5. Energy
6. Health and Human Services
7. Housing and Urban Development
8. The Interior
9. Justice
10. Labor
11. State
12. Transportation
13. The Treasury
14. Veterans Affairs

The next chapter explains each of these departments.

Chapter 5

The Executive Departments

*D*epartment of Agriculture
The Department of Agriculture was created in 1862. It affects all Americans because it is concerned with the food they eat. The Agriculture Department works to help stop hunger and malnutrition. It helps farmers get a fair price for their crops, and it arranges for them to sell their produce in other countries. The department also inspects meat, eggs, and other food products to make sure they are of good quality.

The Agriculture Department also works to help landowners protect soil, water, forests, and other natural resources. This is good for the environment, and it helps the country to produce more food.

The Department of Agriculture runs a big educational program to teach farmers about the latest developments in agricultural science and technology. It also directs nutrition studies and home economics research.

The Food and Drug Administration, a part of the Department of Agriculture, is responsible for maintaining the quality of the food and drugs Americans consume.

Veterinarians employed by the Department of Agriculture routinely inspect living conditions for animals that will be slaughtered for food.

Department of Commerce

The Department of Commerce was created in 1913 to help improve the United States economy. It does research in science, engineering, and other technology, and it provides business and government planners with statistics on social and economic issues. This department also helps minority businesses to grow.

Within the Department of Commerce are several bureaus. The Industry and Trade Administration is the bureau that helps manufacturing and trade. Another bureau, the Maritime Administration, helps American shipping. The Patent and Trademark Office registers inventions and issues patents and trademarks. The Census Bureau takes a count of American citizens every ten years and provides information on how Americans live. The National Bureau of Standards

Under the Constitution, every ten years the federal government must undertake to count all U.S. citizens. The numbers gathered are then used to apportion the members of the House of Representatives among the fifty states.

A meteorologist from the National Oceanic and Atmospheric Administration tracks the course of a hurricane in the Pacific Ocean.

makes sure that Americans have a uniform set of weights and measures. And the National Oceanic and Atmospheric Administration reports on the weather in the United States and its territories; it also provides weather forecasts to the general public.

Department of Defense

The Department of Defense, created in 1947, advises the president on all matters involving national defense. It is responsible for providing the military forces needed to protect the United States.

The military forces are the Army, Navy, Marines, and Air Force. Together they have almost two million women and men on active duty. Of these, many thousands, including those on ships at sea, are serving outside the United States. In case of emergency, they can

The Pentagon, the home of the Department of Defense, is the largest office building in the world.

be backed up by more than one million members of the reserve divisions. There are also over a million civilian employees in the Defense Department.

The central office of this department is at the Pentagon, the world's largest office building, in Washington, D.C. Each state also has some defense activities.

Department of Education

The Department of Education decides who should receive educational assistance from the government. This includes money, advice, and other kinds of aid. Educational programs used to be run by the Department of Health, Education and Welfare, but that changed in 1979 when the Department of Education was created.

Included in the Education Department are agencies that cover all levels of education from nursery school to graduate school, plus bilingual, private, vocational, and adult education.

This adult education supervisor in St. Joseph, Missouri, works with two returning students who are working toward a high school equivalency diploma. The Department of Education is concerned with education at all levels.

Department of Energy

Created in 1977, the Department of Energy looks for new sources of energy and tries to find new ways of using energy.

This department is also responsible for selling the electrical power generated by some government dams. It sets fuel prices and controls the use of certain energy sources. It also

Nuclear power facilities such as this one in Kentucky are monitored by the Department of Energy.

monitors the nuclear power program. If there is a fuel shortage, the Department of Energy is in charge of the rationing program.

Department of Health and Human Services

The Department of Health and Human Services, founded in 1953, is one of the biggest departments in the executive branch. It affects the lives of all Americans, from newborn babies to the oldest citizens.

One of its best-known agencies is the Social Security Administration. This agency collects taxes from workers and pays out living expenses to the elderly and to the widowed parents of dependent children. Another agency is the Public Health Service, which is headed by the surgeon general. Its job is to protect and improve the health of the American

Surgeon General Jocelyn Elders heads the Public Health Service.

people. The Office of Human Development Services deals with problems of certain groups, such as children of low-income families.

Until 1979, the Department of Health and Human Services was called the Department of Health, Education and Welfare.

Department of Housing and Urban Development

The Department of Housing and Urban Development (HUD) was formed in 1965 to improve the quality of life for people who live in America's cities. HUD guarantees that the mortgages on homes will be repaid, so that families can buy houses. It helps to pay the rent of people who cannot afford decent housing, and it gives loans to the elderly and the handicapped for building or repairing housing projects. HUD helps to rebuild neighborhoods by giving grants to states and communities for their community development activities. This department also runs programs to fight discrimination in housing.

The Department of Housing and Urban Development works with local munic-
ipalities to improve conditions in cities. Here a garden is being tended in New
York City.

Department of the Interior

The Department of the Interior was formed in 1849 to protect our natural resources. The United States owns millions of acres of land and natural resources. These are for the enjoyment of the American people.

The Department of the Interior creates policies to help protect the country's land, water, fish, and animals. One agency of the department is the National Parks Service, which helps to preserve the forests and historical places in America's national parks. It also encourages Americans to visit and appreciate these places.

This department also checks mineral resources to make sure they are used in ways that will benefit all of the American people.

The Department of the Interior develops policies concerning American Indians, too, and is responsible for more than two hundred Indian reservations. It is also responsible for people who live in America's island territories in the Caribbean Sea and the Pacific Ocean.

Yellowstone National Park in Wyoming is an immense area of natural beauty and resources.

Department of Justice

The Department of Justice can be considered the largest law firm in the nation. This is true because the Justice Department gives legal advice and opinions to the executive branch, and because it defends the government in cases brought against it.

The Justice Department was created in 1870 and is headed by the United States attorney general. It has thousands of lawyers, investigators, and agents. It protects consumers by prosecuting people and companies that break federal laws. This department also supervises jails and enforces civil rights laws that affect voting, education, employment, housing, and use of public facilities.

Perhaps the two best-known agencies in the Department of Justice are the Federal Bureau of Investigation (FBI) and the Immigration and Naturalization Service (INS). The FBI gathers and reports facts, locates witnesses, and collects evidence of crimes against the United States government. The INS is in charge of allowing immigrants to come into the United States, and deciding which of them will become citizens. It also guards the country's borders to prevent illegal

The Immigration and Naturalization Service oversees the movement of visitors and immigrants across the country's borders. This photo on the right is from the early twentieth century, when millions of people moved to the United States.

entry. Most branches of the Department of Justice have offices in all major cities.

Department of Labor

The Department of Labor was formed in 1913 to help all Americans who need and want to work. The Labor Department tries to improve working conditions and to enhance people's chances of getting work. It does this by making sure that all employers obey the federal labor laws.

These labor laws guarantee every worker's right to safe and healthful working conditions. The laws also ensure a minimum hourly wage, overtime pay, and freedom from employment discrimination. They provide unemployment insurance benefits to workers who lose their jobs, and workers' compensation payments when workers are ill and cannot work.

The Department of Labor also gives special help to older and younger workers and to minorities, women, and the disabled.

One agency of the Department of Labor is the Bureau of Labor Statistics, which gathers facts and figures about the country's workers. Another agency, the Occupational Safety and Health Administration, develops standards for safe and healthful working conditions and makes sure employers observe them.

The Department of Labor was formed in 1913, in part to stop industry's practice of exploiting child labor (top). Today, Occupational Safety and Health Administration officers (left) inspect work sites to ensure safe conditions for America's workforce.

Department of State

Founded way back in 1789, the Department of State is responsible for relations between the United States and other

The United Nations in New York City is home to diplomats from around the world. The United States has representatives from the State Department to speak on behalf of the U.S. government.

countries. The State Department runs all of the American embassies and consulates in foreign countries. Working in these embassies are hundreds of diplomats and members of an agency of the department called the Foreign Service.

The State Department is also involved in making treaties and agreements with foreign nations. And representatives of the department speak for the United States in the United Nations and in more than fifty other international organizations.

Department of Transportation

The Department of Transportation was established in 1966 to set up this country's transportation programs and policies.

Within the department are several agencies. One of them, the Federal Highway Administration, plans the construction of interstate highways and lays down safety rules for roads built by the government. Another agency, the Federal Aviation Administration, is in charge of airplane safety. The Federal Railroad Administration regulates the nation's railways and makes sure they operate safely.

The Coast Guard is part of the Transportation Department during peacetime and part of the Defense Department during war. It patrols the country's coastal waters to prevent piracy and smuggling, and it is involved in search-and-rescue operations on water.

The interstate highway system that links all parts of the lower forty-eight states was funded through the Department of Transportation.

The Bureau of Engraving and Printing, a part of the Treasury Department, prints all of the United States' paper currency and postage stamps.

Department of the Treasury

The Department of the Treasury, created in 1789, has only four main responsibilities, but they are very big ones: (1) it makes and recommends policies on spending and taxes; (2) it serves as financial agent for the United States government; (3) it enforces laws; and (4) it manufactures coins and currency.

The Internal Revenue Service is a division of the Treasury Department that enforces all laws having to do with taxation. The Bureau of the Mint makes coins. The Bureau of Engraving and Printing prints all paper money, bonds, and government checks.

The Secret Service, which guards the president, the vice president, and their families, is also part of the Department of the Treasury.

The Treasury Department also tracks down forgers and counterfeiters of American money and securities.

Department of Veterans Affairs

The Department of Veterans Affairs, created in 1930, operates programs to benefit people who have served in the armed forces. It makes payments to families whose members are disabled or killed during military service. It also pays out pensions to retired military personnel, and it is responsible for the education and rehabilitation of veterans. The department runs a medical care program for veterans and has its own nursing homes, clinics, and medical centers.

As you can see, the executive branch of our government has a very big job. But even though the United States is a large country, its system of government was designed to be simple.

Although the executive branch is itself very large, it has a simple structure. This is why the president of the United States and all of the president's advisers are able to make sure that the nation runs smoothly, that its citizens are taken care of, and that it keeps up its relationships with other countries.

For Further Reading

Green, Carl and William Sanford. *Presidency.* Vero Beach, Fla.: Rourke Corporation, 1990.

Parker, Nancy W. *President's Cabinet and How It Grows.* New York: HarperCollins Children's Books, 1991

Pious, Richard M. *The Presidency.* Englewood Cliffs, N.J.: Silver Burdett Press, 1991.

Index

About the Author

Diane Patrick writes books for young readers and is a freelance writer of music reviews and profiles of musicians. Her music reviews have appeared in music magazines including *Billboard*, *Jazziz*, *JazzTimes*, and *Wire*. For Franklin Watts, Ms. Patrick has written *Martin Luther King, Jr.* and *Coretta Scott King*. The latter was chosen by the New York Public Library for its "Books For the Teenage" list. Ms. Patrick lives in New York City.